IDEAL AND REALITY IN THE FICTIONAL NARRATIVES OF THEOPHILE GAUTIER

by Albert B. Smith

UNIVERSITY OF FLORIDA PRESS / GAINESVILLE 1969

Library of Congress
Catalog Card No. 79-81256

PRINTED BY THE STORTER PRINTING COMPANY
GAINESVILLE, FLORIDA

NOTE

I use frequently in this study the collection of Gautier's *contes fantastiques* published by Corti in 1962, since the shorter narratives of the ideal appear here in an easily accessible, recent edition. References to narratives in this collection will be indicated by the abbreviation *CF*, and the page number(s). For other pertinent works I have gone to the latest available edition.

My essay is the outgrowth of an inquiry into Gautier's fiction undertaken two years ago in preparation for a course on French Romanticism. The first fruit of my reading was an article, "The Changing Ideal in Two of Gautier's Fictional Narratives," forthcoming in *Romanic Review*. The monograph was completed thanks to a grant from the

University of Florida Humanities Council. I should like to take this opportunity to express publicly to the Council my deep appreciation. I should further like to thank my colleagues, Frieda S. Brown, Claude K. Abraham, and Raymond Gay-Crosier, for their criticism of the manuscript and for their valuable suggestions. Thanks also go to Professor J. Wayne Conner, Chairman of the Department of Romance Languages, University of Florida, for his encouragement throughout our association. Finally, I owe special thanks to my wife Rita, not only for the long hours she has spent typing the different drafts but also—and most of all—for her presence.

This essay is dedicated to all the faithful.

A.B.S.

January, 1969

CONTENTS

1. INTRODUCTION

Recent scholarly interest in Théophile Gautier's prose fiction has produced valuable and suggestive insights into the man and his work. Georges Poulet in *Etudes sur le temps humain* (Paris, 1949) uses certain stories and novels to support his characterization of Gautier as a man desperately in search of an answer to the threat of mortality.[1] Elsewhere he cites prose works in a study of Gautier's romanticism.[2] P.-G. Castex gives a long chapter to Gautier in his book on the major authors of *contes fantastiques* in the nineteenth century.[3] While he is naturally concerned with questions of genre and sources, Castex considers Gautier's fantastic tales primarily as expressions of secret desires and torments. Albert J. George studies Gautier's place in the development of short fiction in France during the first half of the nineteenth century.[4] Professor George thus focuses on form, structure, and technique in Gautier's works. He is only secondarily interested in the man, but he, too, asserts that Gautier often put himself into his narratives, articulating under the disguise of his heroes certain hopes and fears. Marcel Schneider, like Castex, studies Gautier as an author of *contes fantastiques*.[5] While the burden of his presentation is on the formal aspects of Gautier's narratives, Schneider agrees that certain stories reflect Gautier's inner life and are expressions of secret, even unrecognized problems which afflicted him.

1. Pages 278–307.
2. *Trois essais de mythologie romantique* (Paris, 1966), pp. 83–134.
3. *Le Conte fantastique en France de Nodier à Maupassant* (Paris, 1951), pp. 214–47.
4. *Short Fiction in France, 1800–1850* (Syracuse, 1964), pp. 166–88.
5. *La Littérature fantastique en France* (Paris, 1964), pp. 213–21.

Such concentration on Gautier's prose fiction, especially on his lesser-known narratives, is well justified. If knowledge of Gautier remains limited, part of the blame must be laid to careless or incomplete consideration of his fictional works. The themes of ideal and of reality, for example, have not received the attention they deserve. Although critics have recognized in Gautier the prominence of the search for an ideal and of antipathy toward present reality,[6] they have not studied these questions fully where he treats them most elaborately, in his fictional narratives. Jasinski's inquiry into Gautier's early career does not go beyond the time of *Mademoiselle de Maupin*. Questions of genre so restrict even Castex and Schneider that they do not consider a number of narratives dealing with the quest of an ideal. Other critical works suffer from similar shortcomings, so that our knowledge of ideal and reality in Gautier's work is defective.

The present essay takes a step toward correcting this situation. By analyzing the representations of the ideal and of reality in Gautier's fictional narratives, I intend to demonstrate that these questions are far more complex than is generally thought. Readers have tended to associate Gautier with an ideal of perfect beauty.[7] The narratives show that he cannot be so neatly tagged. Between 1831 and 1865 Gautier wrote more than a dozen works—short stories, novelettes, and novels—primarily concerned with the quest of an ideal.[8] What char-

6. See, for example, René Jasinski, *Les Années romantiques de Th. Gautier* (Paris, 1929), p. 303.

7. See René Lauret, "L'Ame romantique de Théophile Gautier," *MdF*, CXI (1911), 232; Paul Bourget, "L'Art de Théophile Gautier," *Pages de critique et de doctrine* (Paris, 1912), I, 78; Henriette E. A. Velthuis, *Théophile Gautier: l'homme, l'artiste* (Middleburg, 1924), p. 171, et passim; Louise B. Dillingham, *The Creative Imagination of Théophile Gautier: A Study in Literary Psychology*, Psychological Monographs, XXXVII, No. 1 (1927), 331, 337; Antoine-Orliac, "Essai sur le pessimisme chez les Parnassiens," *MdF*, CCVI (1928), 10–11; H. van der Tuin, *L'Evolution psychologique, esthétique et littéraire de Théophile Gautier* (Paris, 1933), pp. 119–23; John A. Guischard, *Le Conte fantastique au XIXe siècle* (Montréal, 1947), p. 93; Joanna Richardson, *Théophile Gautier: His Life and Times* (New York, 1959), p. 287.

8. *La Cafetière* (1831); *Omphale, histoire rococo* (1834); *Mademoiselle de Maupin* (1835); *La Morte amoureuse* (1836); *Fortunio* (1837); *La Pipe d'opium* (1838); *La Toison d'or* (1839); *Le Pied de momie*

acterizes these works, as a body, is the evident evolution in the character of the ideal presented. It is true that the early ideal is one of beauty; we see this in *Mademoiselle de Maupin.* But later stories show Gautier's heroes seeking happiness elsewhere. A similar change is visible in the representations of present reality. According to the narratives, present reality is a manifold concept. At different points between 1831 and 1865 different aspects predominate as threats to the idealist's quest. It is apparent furthermore that changes in the nature of the ideal have a direct bearing upon those elements of reality which Gautier's heroes at given points feel to be a hindrance to their quest.

It will be my task here to define the character of the ideal as it changes in the prose works and to clarify the nature of reality and its relationship to the idealist's quest. To do this does not demand a full analysis of every narrative. The changes which take place are most clearly demonstrable from single representative works from each of three major moments in the evolution of the ideal. All of the narratives, however, have their place in this development. Certain ones naturally group themselves around the early ideal, others around the later ideals. I shall therefore pay primary attention to *Mademoiselle de Maupin* (1835), *Arria Marcella* (1852), and *Spirite* (1865) as key works among Gautier's representations, using less elaborate narratives from each general period to support my demonstrations.

Our notions of ideal and reality derive from the characters in each story and the contexts in which they appear. Understanding a particular narrative demands, therefore, that we establish to what end Gautier combines these elements. No one up to now has approached the narratives from this angle. This is the most probable reason for failures to get beneath their surface.

(1840); *Le Chevalier double* (1840); *Deux acteurs pour un rôle* (1841); *Le Club des hachichins* (1846); *Arria Marcella* (1852); *Avatar* (1856); *Jettatura* (1856); *Le Roman de la momie* (1857); *Spirite* (1865).

Hero and heroine are more than ordinarily important, for it is they who symbolize idealist and ideal, respectively. Two types of heroes predominate. One is a young man who, suddenly introduced to a new order of reality, perceives in it the promise of heretofore unknown felicity and seeks to achieve lasting union with his newly found source of pleasure. Romuald, of *La Morte amoureuse,* is a representative example. Reared in a seminary, without any knowledge of the secular world, he conceives of no greater happiness than serving God as a priest. On the day of his ordination, however, he encounters the extraordinarily beautiful courtesan Clarimonde, whose invitation to join her for a life of eroticism and worldly pleasure awakens his latent sensuality. *La Morte amoureuse* is the story of his almost fatal attempt to achieve happiness with Clarimonde without sacrificing his chances for salvation.

The second type is a young man who has already sensed the happiness promised by the "other" reality and whose life is dedicated to the search for that ideal. D'Albert, of *Mademoiselle de Maupin,* has conceived an ideal of beauty which it is his consuming desire to see realized. Likewise, Octavien, in *Arria Marcella,* disgusted with the world around him, seeks to achieve union with the spirits of famous women from the past who represent charms which modern reality cannot accord.

Certain constants recur in Gautier's representations of all these heroes. In the three examples given above, there is implicit a serious conflict between present reality and the pleasures envisioned in the ideal. In some cases, it is simply the failure of the former to offer the happiness promised by the latter. In other cases, present reality represents a very real threat to attainment to the ideal. Implicit furthermore is the direction of the hero's quest. Most of Gautier's heroes move more *toward* the ideal than away from reality. They are primarily intent on attaining to that "other" reality which they conceive in the distance. If there is any question of escape from the present, it is above all because they feel that the world around them is trying to hold them back. The quest is, in addition, extraordinarily intense. D'Albert thinks of nothing else than his ideal and would be willing to give up his life to enjoy a moment of union with it. Octave de Saville, of *Avatar,* is likewise willing to risk death in his attempt to possess the woman of his desires.

Gautier's heroes, then, are intent seekers after some object in lasting union with which they expect to achieve supreme happiness. Their attitude toward present reality is negative, for they know that it is an obstacle to their quest. Yet, aside from these general resemblances, they undergo significant changes of orientation. Octavien's approach is different from d'Albert's; Malivert's approach in *Spirite* represents an advance over that of Octavien. We shall see later that these changes have a direct relation to the evolving nature of the ideal.

As focal point of the hero's love, the heroine symbolizes the ideal. His desire to possess her represents the idealist's desire to attain to lasting union with what he considers the ultimate good. D'Albert is explicit in recognizing Madelaine de Maupin as his ideal incarnate. In sexual union with her he achieves the highest level of happiness he can imagine. But erotic satisfaction is not his primary concern. He has known intimately other women, in none of whom has he been able to find the unique complex of qualities which make up his ideal and which Madelaine de Maupin so abundantly possesses. She sums up all of the elements which he conceives to comprise beauty. Similarly Clarimonde embodies a complex of attributes which all go to make up Romuald's ideal.

As the hero's orientation evolves through the different stories, so does the nature of the heroine. Each significant change thus represents a change in the overall character of the ideal at a given moment. By identifying the elements which make up the heroine's character at the beginning and in successive narratives, we shall be tracing the evolution of the ideal.

A third personage appearing in the narratives is the guide. While this character does not figure in every story, his role is important whenever Gautier does introduce him. It is his task to lead the hero in the direction which he, the guide, is convinced to be most salutary for the well-being of his ward. In most of the narratives he is unsympathetic, for he attempts to draw the hero away from his quest of the ideal. Father Sérapion, in *La Morte amoureuse,* is Romuald's self-appointed religious guide. Recognizing Clarimonde's threat to Romuald's spiritual welfare, Sérapion warns the young priest to beware of the risks involved in sensual passion. As Romuald's desire grows, Sérapion redoubles his efforts to save his ward. He is finally successful, but the measure he employs is extreme—destruction of Clarimonde—so that the young sensualist can view him only as a monster, not as an apostle of the Church.

Most of Gautier's guides symbolize aspects of the outside world which the heroes recognize are obstructing their quest. Knowledge of the guide's character in a given work therefore helps us to understand better the nature of ambient reality as represented in the narratives. By determining why he is repugnant, we can see what specifically in the environment is felt to be antithetical to the ideal.

The same may be said for the more important secondary characters. The role of some underscores the idea that the world around the idealist can only be a defective source of pleasure. Such is the function of Rosette in *Mademoiselle de Maupin.* For d'Albert she represents a compromise with reality. Despairing of ever realizing his ideal of beauty, he attempts to find in a liaison with the most charming woman in his circle as high a degree of satisfaction as possible. Rosette does in fact go some way towards giving him the extreme measure of delight which he demands, but he recognizes that she is far from being an incarnation of his ideal: "J'éprouve à côté de Rosette ce calme plat et cette espèce de bien-être paresseux qui résulte de la satisfaction des sens, mais rien de plus: et ce n'est pas assez!"[9] Even the most charming aspects of ambient reality cannot compare with the pleasures envisioned in the ideal.

9. *Mademoiselle de Maupin,* ed. Adolphe Boschot, nouvelle éd. (Paris [1955]), p. 132. Subsequent references to *Mademoiselle de Maupin* will be to this edition.

In other secondary personages we see again the restrictive action characteristic of the environment. Katy, in *Deux acteurs pour un rôle,* wants the aspiring young actor Henrich to give up the stage for the more comfortable existence of pastor and father. Mme d'Ymbercourt of *Spirite* symbolizes the material world ever at pains to pin down the idealist and arrest his impulsion toward the ideal. When she calls Malivert away from meditation on the possibility that he may be in contact with the supernatural world, Gautier points out that "le réel essayait de reconquérir sa proie sur l'idéal."[10]

By examining context, too, we may gain additional understanding of the character of the ideal and of the idealist's attitude toward reality. The majority of the narratives belong to the *genre fantastique,* or to be more strict, the *pseudo-fantastique,* characterized, according to Roger Caillois, by the protagonist's encounter with apparently impossible events which turn out to have been visions perceived in a dream.[11] In a number of stories Gautier represents his hero actually enjoying possession of his ideal, but in a dream state. What the hero desires thus comes true, or rather *seems to,* for the dichotomy between real world and world of dream is sharp, and the former cannot provide the pleasures inherent in the latter. In *Omphale,* for example, the narrator by way of dream receives instruction in the delights of eroticism offered by a charming young marquise come to apparent life from a Regency tapestry. After his introduction to love he can scarcely contain himself by day for anticipation of the thrills which he experiences by night.

Two other works, *La Pipe d'opium* and *Le Club des hachichins,* are much like the dream stories in that they describe events in which the narrator participates while in an irrational state, produced in these two cases by drugs. On the surface these narratives are simple reports of hallucinatory experi-

10. *Spirite,* 3e éd. (Paris, 1872), p. 29. Subsequent references to *Spirite* will be to this edition.

11. Preface to *Fantastique: soixante récits de terreur* (Paris, 1958), p. 5. See also Caillois, "De la féerie à la science fiction," *Anthologie du fantastique* (Paris, 1966), I, 12.

ences; but considered in relation to the other stories of the ideal, they appear to be structured with particular aims in view. As in the dream accounts, the narrators enjoy pleasures which everyday reality is incapable of providing, and they frequently call attention to the antagonism between the delights of the hallucinatory state and the drabness of real life.

Dream stories and reports of hallucination thus have two functions in regard to the ideal. Gautier uses them as a device both to characterize the ideal and to define ambient reality. By analyzing what gives the hero or narrator pleasure in his supposedly irrational state, we can determine his affection at a given moment. And by attention to the real context in which he exists and which appears as antagonistic to the dream world, we are able to establish more firmly what aspects of reality constitute a threat to the ultimate happiness sought in the ideal.

The context of other narratives is more realistic in nature. The events which take place in *Mademoiselle de Maupin* are presented as if they actually had happened. There is no dream, no hallucination. Likewise, *La Toison d'or* is a traditional fictional account without any ostensibly impossible events which suddenly rend the fabric of ordinary reality. Nevertheless these realistic representations display the same elements which we may regard as characteristic of ideal and reality in Gautier's stories: the ideal is a good which promises supreme happiness, while the real world is an evil which seriously threatens the hero's quest and from which he is constantly at pains to escape.

More closely related to the ideal than to reality is another question of context, the location of the ideal in respect to the idealist. Where Gautier's hero situates his ideal is an important point for, as will become evident later, the locale in which the ideal resides changes radically in both space and time.

Finally, the outcome of the stories conditions the conclusions which we draw regarding the different orientations. Most of the narratives are stories of failure. A hero, once introduced to the ideal, may enjoy it briefly, but in the end he reawakens to present reality (*La Cafetière*). Or his enjoyment is disrupted by some force originating in the real world (*La Morte amoureuse*). Or he may lose his chance to possess the ideal even before he touches it (*Avatar*). Whatever happens, he experiences such intense regret that he can never henceforth be happy. Nor can he recapture his ideal if contact is once broken. Madelaine de Maupin, after giving d'Albert a single night of bountiful love, disappears forever; Octavien finds it impossible to recreate his moment of oneiric felicity with Arria Marcella.

Only in *Spirite,* the last of Gautier's narratives of the ideal, does the hero achieve success. Once aware of the "other" reality, he strives after it single-mindedly, overcoming all forces of present reality which attempt to hold him back, until in the end he gains lasting possession of his ideal. This fact of final success, as compared with so many accounts of failure, must have meaning. The denouement of each narrative implies a judgment as to the efficacy of the means which the hero employs to attain to his ideal. It is for the reader to perceive that judgment. Thus the outcome of the narratives is as important as character and context in helping us to understand the evolution in the nature of the ideal and in conditioning our evaluation of the changes. That changes do occur is manifest. Let us now see what they are.

2. THE IDEAL

Proper consideration of the ideal demands that we know how Gautier understands the term. Two definitions from Robert's dictionary will help to clarify this usage: "2° Ce qu'on se représente ou se propose comme type parfait ou modèle absolu dans l'ordre pratique, esthétique ou intellectuel .... 4° Ce qui, dans quelque ordre que ce soit, donnerait une parfaite satisfaction aux aspirations du cœur ou de l'esprit (*par oppos. à la* décevante réalité)."[1] The major difference between these definitions is in the nature of the two kinds of ideal defined. In 2° it exists only in the idealist's mind. It is an idea, a conception, a representation of an absolute. An example would be the notion we might have of perfect beauty.

Robert's second definition (4°) assumes that the ideal could exist as fact. According to 4°, then, it is more than a conception. It has a derivative relationship to a conception but, as far as the idealist is concerned, it is susceptible of discovery or realization. Indeed union with the realized ideal is precisely what the idealist desires. We may thus imagine a man conceiving of a perfect good, then seeking to find that good in tangible form. While it might not exist at the moment (Robert's use of *donnerait* suggests a presently unreal condition), the idealist would consider possession of it within the realm of possibility. If he did discover it, he would, according to 4°, experience at last the perfect satisfaction to which he aspired.

Gautier uses *idéal* in both of the senses allowed by Robert. The ideal in the narratives is first a conception, perfect beauty, for example. But it is also an object (taken in the broadest

1. Paul Robert, *Dictionnaire alphabétique et analogique de la langue française* (Paris, 1951–64), III, 595.

sense of the term), one embodying whatever features go to make up the original preconception. As an object, the ideal is considered to exist somewhere. While its occurrence may be rare, it is nevertheless felt by Gautier's heroes to be within the scope of possibility if not of probability. Else they would not be so hopeful as they are. It is furthermore envisioned as a source of perfect satisfaction, indeed of supreme happiness. Gautier's idealist knows that by coming together with his ideal he will achieve ultimate felicity. Whether he can maintain union with the ideal as long as he desires is another question.

The Early Ideal

Mademoiselle de Maupin (1835) is apparently the work on which scholars and critics have based their assertions that Gautier's ideal was one of beauty, for beauty is precisely what Gautier's hero-idealist d'Albert seeks. Yet there is beauty and beauty, and our understanding of it, at least insofar as the narratives are concerned, is imperfect. An analysis of *Mademoiselle de Maupin* and of other early narratives will help us to clarify this point.

D'Albert has a preconception of beauty so perfect that nothing in reality has ever equaled it. Though he has had it since childhood, he has no idea of how or where it originated. The terms which he uses to characterize it are reminiscent of Platonism. Whenever he speaks of beauty, it is as of an abstraction. He situates it in some ethereal region (p. 239) where he imagines it to reside as an eternal essence (p. 315). Rosette recognizes that d'Albert's very character turns on this notion of essential beauty: "Quelque chose l'attire et l'appelle invinciblement qui n'est pas de ce monde ni en ce monde, et il ne peut avoir de repos ni jour ni nuit; et, comme l'héliotrope dans une cave, il se tord pour se tourner vers le soleil, qu'il ne voit pas. —C'est un de ces hommes dont l'âme n'a pas été trempée assez complètement dans les eaux du Léthé avant d'être liée à son corps, et qui garde du ciel dont elle vient des réminiscences d'éternelle beauté qui la travaillent et la tourmentent, qui se souvient qu'elle a eu des ailes, et qui n'a plus que des pieds" (p. 155).

But, if d'Albert's *conception* is of an essence, his *desire* is that that essence be incarnated. What he wants first and foremost is to see his ideal realized in the here and now. Time and again he makes explicit that he will not be satisfied until he can see and touch the *embodiment* of the eternal essence which he conceives (pp. 62, 181, et passim). The mark of his orientation is thus its fundamental materialism. It is not enough to know that beauty exists somewhere as an essence; to give full pleasure, it must be enjoyed physically. His problem, therefore, is to find a woman who embodies his notion of beauty. For it must be a woman. In an earlier age, he would have sought the image of the perfection he desires in the hermaphrodite (p. 201). But that age is past. Such perfect beauty can no more be hoped for in men; a vestige of it can be found only in women (p. 315).

No woman anywhere, however, meets d'Albert's stringent requirements. From the early pages of the novel Gautier shows him on the verge of despair at the thought he may never see his preconception realized. When he at last confronts its incarnation in Madelaine de Maupin, he is of course delighted beyond all his expectations (p. 256).

D'Albert's ideal, in a general sense, will therefore be the living concretization of a preconceived archetype. What he is looking for more particularly is beauty of form, which for him depends upon perfect harmony: "La beauté, c'est l'harmonie, et une personne également laide partout est souvent moins désagréable à regarder qu'une femme inégalement belle" (p. 134). All parts of the whole must *fit* to absolute perfection in order to give the pleasure which the young idealist demands. Madelaine de Maupin embodies just this perfection: "Tout était réuni dans le beau corps qui posait devant lui: —délicatesse et force, forme et couleur, les lignes d'une statue grecque du meilleur temps et le ton d'un Titien. —Il voyait là, palpable et cristallisée, la nuageuse chimère qu'il avait tant de fois essayé d'arrêter dans son vol: —il n'était pas forcé, comme il s'en plaignait si amèrement à son ami Silvio, de circonscrire ses regards sur une certaine portion assez bien faite, et de ne la point dépasser, sous peine de voir quelque chose d'effroyable, et son œil amoureux descendait de la tête aux pieds et remontait des pieds à la tête, toujours doucement caressé par une forme harmonieuse et correcte" (p. 366).

That the words *harmony* and *perfection* are such imprecise terms should not trouble us. It would take a statue of the female body, nay, a materialization of Madelaine de Maupin herself, to give us an exact idea of what d'Albert conceives perfect harmony to be. Even at that, there might well be disagreement among viewers as to what actually constitutes harmony. Perfection of any kind is ultimately an individual notion. Da Vinci, in the well-known diagram he made of the supposedly perfect human body, had his idea, and there is no guarantee that d'Albert—or anyone else—would see physical beauty in exactly the same way. It is enough to know that for d'Albert beauty resides in a woman whose proportions he personally finds supremely attractive.

It is evident in *Mademoiselle de Maupin* that d'Albert's materialism depends primarily upon appeal to the senses of sight and touch. When the disguised Madelaine first appears to him in female dress, his appreciation goes exclusively to the plastic aspect; and his consideration of the best artistic mediums for rendering such beauty reflects the strength of his visual and tactile inclinations: "J'ai fait vingt sonnets sur ces épaules-là, mais ce n'est point assez: je voudrais quelque chose que je pusse toucher du doigt et qui fût exactement pareil; les vers ne rendent que le fantôme de la beauté et non la beauté elle-même. Le peintre arrive à une apparence plus exacte, mais ce n'est qu'une apparence. La sculpture a toute la réalité que peut avoir une chose complètement fausse; elle a l'aspect multiple, porte ombre, et se laisse toucher" (p. 257).

D'Albert's sensibilities are not limited, however, to sight and touch. Underlying his esthetic appreciations is a broad sensuous disposition. Pleasure for him is to be derived from stimulation of all the senses. While the visual and the tactile predominate, he is also enthusiastically responsive to auditory and olfactory stimuli. His account of a pleasant dream lists flowers, the singing of birds, sunlight, warmth—all aspects of the milieu—which combined to produce in him a feeling of felicity. His conclusions reflect the breadth of his sensuousness: "On a beau faire: le bonheur est blanc et rose; on ne peut guère le représenter autrement. Les couleurs tendres lui reviennent de droit. —Il n'a sur sa palette que du vert d'eau, du bleu de ciel et du jaune paille: ses tableaux sont tout dans le clair comme ceux des peintres chinois. —Des fleurs, de la lumière, des parfums, une peau soyeuse et douce qui touche la vôtre, une harmonie voilée et qui vient on ne sait d'où, on est parfaitement heureux avec cela; il n'y a pas moyen d'être heureux différemment" (p. 123). He is unequivocal in declaring that beauty for him does not reside exclusively in plastic appeal: "L'air, le geste, la démarche, le souffle, la couleur, le son, le parfum, tout ce qui est la vie entre pour moi dans la composition de la beauté; tout ce qui embaume, chante ou rayonne y revient de droit" (p. 135).

What d'Albert ultimately seeks through materialism is supreme happiness. Whatever touches his senses must bring the required joy to his spirit, a feeling of ecstasy akin to that rapture which we associate with the experience of Christian mystics. His feelings, however, will have nothing to do with Christianity. In fact he rejects the Christian outlook as too spiritualistic, its focus being on intangible goods, and opposes to it pagan delight in the beauties of this life. His soul must be stirred, but only by a divinity which becomes tangible. Thus his admiration for Venus instead of the Christian Virgin: "La Vénus sort de la mer pour aborder au monde, —comme il convient à une divinité qui aime les hommes, —toute nue et toute seule. —Elle préfère la terre à l'Olympe et a pour amants plus d'hommes que de dieux: elle ne s'enveloppe pas des voiles langoureux de la mysticité; elle se tient debout, son dauphin derrière elle, le pied sur sa conque de nacre; le soleil frappe sur son ventre poli, et de sa blanche main elle soutient en l'air les flots de ses beaux cheveux où le vieux père Océan a semé ses perles les plus parfaites. —On la peut voir: elle ne cache rien, car la pudeur n'est faite que pour les laides, et c'est une invention moderne, fille du mépris chrétien de la forme et de la matière" (p. 193). Madelaine de Maupin he sees as just such a divinity: the essence of beauty incarnate (p. 315).

Mademoiselle de Maupin is not the only narrative that manifests this kind of materialism. In *La Morte amoureuse* (1836) Clarimonde symbolizes an ideal much like that which d'Albert finds realized in Madelaine de Maupin. Clarimonde is extraordinarily beautiful, more so than the most outstanding creations of either poets or painters. Every feature is perfect. She has the air of a goddess. Romuald observes that, by her beauty, she cannot be an ordinary woman; she must be some supernatural creature (*CF*, p. 82).

His appreciation of her shows the same concern with physical beauty that characterizes d'Albert. What stirs Romuald most when he first sees Clarimonde is the external aspect—her perfect features and her magnificent robe—which he fondly describes in great detail (*CF*, pp. 82-83). Later, when called to stand vigil over her corpse, he cannot pray because his attention is constantly drawn back to the charming contour beneath the shroud (*CF*, p. 97). When she returns to him in his dreams, it is her physical attractiveness that holds his attention (*CF*, p. 103).

While the term *sensual,* rather than *sensuous,* might better be applied to Romuald's orientation, it nevertheless partakes of the same materialism which characterizes d'Albert. Romuald imagines in his dream life with Clarimonde that he is enjoying the most exciting pleasures. They reside in a rich palace in Venice, surrounded by art objects of the greatest worth. The quality of Romuald's existence is that of a prince. He dresses in the richest clothing. He has his own gondola and corps of servants. He frequents the best society; he spends hours gambling (*CF*, p. 109). Everything that Clarimonde has promised him is abundantly appealing to the senses. The erotic pleasures he enjoys with her are extraordinarily rich. As he says, "Elle me rendait mon amour au centuple" (*CF*, p. 110). Indeed all the promises that she has made him are amply fulfilled. In his dream he finds total sensual satisfaction.

La Pipe d'opium (1838) represents the same orientation from a different angle. This is ostensibly an account of Gautier's experiences with opium, but the main interest lies in the desire of a dead girl to be resurrected, so that she may enjoy the worldly pleasures which she missed while alive. In the narrator's expression of her desires it is again materialism that predominates: "elle me raconta qu'elle était morte si jeune, qu'elle ignorait les plaisirs de l'existence, et qu'avant d'aller s'enfoncer pour toujours dans l'immobile éternité, elle voulait jouir de la beauté du monde, s'enivrer de toutes les voluptés et se plonger dans l'océan des joies terrestres; qu'elle se sentait une soif inextinguible de vie et d'amour" (*CF*, p. 130).

While the narrator of *Le Club des hachichins* (1846) does not explicitly state his aims, what he finds in visions produced by hashish clearly coincides with the sensuousness we associate with the early ideal. The chief interest here is in the broadened perceptions afforded by hallucinogens. Gautier's sketch of the legendary Old Man of the Mountain and his Assassins focuses on the intensely pleasurable visions created by hashish and on the sharp contrast between these and the insipidness of real life (*CF*, p. 193). The narrator enjoys brand new experiences, the drug shocking his sensitivity into unexpected responsiveness. His taste is totally transformed, so that water seems like wine and meat like delicious fruit. Objects change their forms. The people around him assume the appearance of birds and bells. The room takes on a new look, everything seeming larger, richer, and infinitely more splendid in an already grandiose milieu (*CF*, pp. 195–97). His sense of hearing is so enhanced that he feels the chords of music performed by one of the guests actually enter his body. Indeed, his own musical capacity is augmented to the point that he has the impression of himself creating the compositions of Weber—and with synesthetic transpositions of sounds into colors! (*CF*, p. 203). His feeling of well-being is extreme. Although he experiences liberation from his body, it is materialistically that he reacts to the ethereal environment in which he seems to find himself: "Une vapeur bleuâtre, un jour élyséen, un reflet de grotte azurine, formaient dans la chambre une atmosphère où je voyais vaguement trembler des contours indécis; cette atmosphère, à la fois fraîche et tiède, humide et parfumée, m'enveloppait, comme l'eau d'un bain, dans un baiser d'une douceur énervante; si je voulais changer de place, l'air caressant faisait autour de moi mille remous voluptueux; une langueur délicieuse s'emparait de mes sens" (*CF*, p. 204).

The Middle Stage

In *Arria Marcella* (1852) Gautier represents a different ideal and a shift in the idealist's attitude which marks a movement away from the earlier materialism. Gautier's hero, Octavien, emphatically declares that nothing in present reality appeals to him. Even the beautiful women he has met he finds surrounded by too many undesirable elements to be perfectly satisfying (*CF*, p. 228). Not only is he not interested in present beauty; he seems in addition to have already recognized the impossibility of fulfilling his desires in the present. What he wants is to enjoy love and beauty *outside* present reality. Thus, he seeks preferably not a real woman but a spirit existing eternally in space and time (*CF*, p. 228). He confirms this in his dream encounter with Arria Marcella: "A mon dégoût des autres femmes ... à la rêverie invincible qui m'entraînait vers ses types radieux au fond des siècles comme des étoiles provocatrices, je comprenais que je n'aimerais jamais que hors du temps et de l'espace" (*CF*, p. 246).

To satisfy his longing, Octavien has turned to history and legend, seeking in famous women from the past, these "sublimes personnifications des désirs et des rêves humains" (*CF*, p. 228), fulfillment of his desires. Like Romuald, Octavien sees his ideal come to life in a dream. Arria Marcella is precisely one of these personifications which he has sought so long, thrillingly beautiful, with every line flawless, as if chiseled by a master sculptor (*CF*, pp. 240–41).

Octavien also finds the microcosm of a whole civilization restored intact to life. In his dream he returns to Pompeii as he conceives it to have been in the days before its destruction. Every house is whole again. The citizens carry on their daily activities as in the past. It is the old city "vivante, jeune, intacte, sur laquelle n'avaient pas coulé les torrents de boue brûlante du Vésuve" (*CF*, p. 232). Octavien is delighted at the unexpected opportunity to return to the Greco-Roman past, and he wastes no time to see all he can. All that he witnesses he admires: the Pompeians' strength, their temperament, their artistic and cultural achievements—their whole way of life. He remarks appreciatively on the robustness of the peasants, contrasting it with the mean aspect of peasants from his own day (*CF*, p. 233). He delights in attending a masterful performance of Plautus' *Casina* presented in an amphitheater whose comforts far surpass anything modern French theaters can offer (*CF*, pp. 237–38). He declares his special esteem for pagan religion, which refused to orient itself toward death and chose, rather, to affirm life enthusiastically, expressing that affirmation everywhere, even in the art work on the sarcophagi and urns of its dead (*CF*, p. 221).

Such admiration for the pagan ethos reveals a continuing materialism. Arria Marcella herself sums up this orientation at the end of the story: "moi, je crois à nos anciens dieux qui aimaient la vie, la jeunesse, la beauté, le plaisir" (*CF*, p. 248). Paganism, as represented here, sought happiness in the joys of the present. In contrast to Christianity it would have no part of spiritual concerns, especially those focused on the afterlife at the expense of this one. So, when Octavien declares his passion for Arria Marcella, he is in effect declaring his sympathy with the fundamental materialism he sees in the pagan approach to life.

This continuing attraction to material pleasures would seem to situate Gautier's story among the early narratives if other factors were not present. First of all, the very fact that Octavien's interest is partly ethical marks a shift from the earlier sensuousness. While materialism is still fundamental in *Arria*

Marcella, it is less exclusive, being accompanied by a strong concern for culture. Octavien may yet display a kinship to d'Albert in his unequivocal appreciation of Arria Marcella's physical charms, but his admiration for Pompeian art and thought reflects a broader disposition. D'Albert had no such cultural interests. That Madelaine de Maupin was supremely beautiful *as an object* sufficed for him. Octavien seeks more.

Octavien's approach and his situation of his ideal in the past do not, moreover, allow an exclusive appeal to the senses. He has no expectation of material enjoyment in the present. Nor can the women whose images he seeks to call up from history and legend ever be materialized. Arria Marcella obviously cannot, in her historical context, be realized, then physically possessed, as is Madelaine de Maupin. By definition, neither she nor the civilization which she represents can be made tangible in the present. Arria Marcella and paganism are spirits and must be loved as such. The idealist's approach cannot be materialistic. Enjoyment of the past can take place only in the imagination. Octavien recognizes this and is convinced that the mind strong enough and properly attuned can resurrect, as it were, the spirit of the past if not the past itself: "En effet, rien ne meurt, tout existe toujours; nulle force ne peut anéantir ce qui fut une fois. Toute action, toute parole, toute forme, toute pensée tombée dans l'océan universel des choses y produit des cercles qui vont s'élargissant jusqu'aux confins de l'éternité. La figuration matérielle ne disparaît que pour les regards vulgaires, et les spectres qui s'en détachent peuplent l'infini .... Quelques esprits passionnés et puissants ont pu amener à eux des siècles écoulés en apparence, et faire revivre des personnages morts pour tous" (*CF*, pp. 245–46).

The historical-cultural interest is already visible in a slight narrative from 1840. In *Le Pied de momie* the narrator travels in dream to Egypt where, visiting the tomb of an ancient pharaoh, he finds a whole civilization preserved intact. The main point of the story is the Egyptian concern for permanence, which shows both in King Xixouthros' evident robustness after thirty centuries and in the contrast which he makes between the durability of his civilization and the transience of more recent civilizations (*CF*, pp. 162–63).

Le Roman de la momie (1857) also belongs to the middle stage in the evolution of the ideal. The frame story resembles *Arria Marcella* in several regards: Evandale's retrospective love for Queen Tahoser, whose history he has found buried in a tomb which he is exploring; his lifelong sadness at being unable to consummate passion for this woman of the past; especially his esteem for the character of Egyptian life, accompanied by his antipathy for what he calls modern "barbarity."

That materialism is still strong is apparent in Evandale's admiration for Egyptian art. As he and his explorers make their way into a tomb, they uncover a number of figurines remarkable for their beauty.[2] Evandale has a particular appreciation for Egyptian architecture, which reflects the ancient ethos, with its sense of grandiosity: "Nous sommes stupidement fiers de quelques ingénieux mécanismes récemment inventés, et nous ne pensons pas aux colossales splendeurs, aux énormités irréalisables pour tout autre peuple de l'antique terre des Pharaons. Nous avons la vapeur; mais la vapeur est moins forte que la pensée qui élevait les pyramides, creusait les hypogées, taillait les montagnes en sphinx, en obélisques, couvrait des salles d'un seul bloc que tous nos engins ne sauraient remuer, ciselait des chapelles monolithes et savait défendre contre le néant la fragile dépouille humaine tant elle avait le sens de l'éternité!" (p. 184).

We have already noticed admiration for this Egyptian "sense of eternity" in *Le Pied de momie.* The figurines discovered in the tomb are still perfectly intact, and the narrator intrudes to note that, as funeral offerings, they are infinitely superior to our modern wreaths, which wilt so quickly. The concern for permanence is also reflected in the mummy itself. The ancient embalmers had done everything possible to pre-

2. *Le Roman de la momie,* précédé de trois contes antiques: *Une Nuit de Cléopâtre, Le Roi Candaule, Arria Marcella,* ed. Adolphe Boschot (Paris, 1963), p. 164. Subsequent references to *Le Roman de la momie* will be to this edition.

serve the body for eternity (p. 180). As Evandale points out, this was an attempt to protect the human body from annihilation by nature (pp. 184, 189). His sympathy with the Egyptian desire to perpetuate physical existence thus reflects that enthusiasm for life which is characteristic of the early and middle orientations.

Also present in Gautier's two stories of Egypt is the same implicit recognition observed in *Arria Marcella* that the historical ideal can be enjoyed only in the imagination. Queen Tahoser sums up, as it were, the civilization of ancient Egypt. To love her, given the context of *Le Roman de la momie,* would be to love the grandiose life and the ethos for which she stands and which Evandale quite evidently admires. But the only way such love can give satisfaction is through an extraordinarily powerful play of the imagination. Octavien displays the ability —once—to so approach the past. If Evandale fails even to make contact with his retrospective ideal, we may blame a personal defect, the incapacity of his imaginative faculty.

The Later Ideal

The last of Gautier's narratives of the ideal is *Spirite* (1865). Castex sees in this novel a strong autobiographical element—Gautier's expression of homage to Carlotta Grisi—and an attempt by Gautier to destroy the image he had for his contemporaries as an inveterate objectivist.[3] This may well be, but there is more; *Spirite* is also the representation of a radically different ideal.

The desires of Gautier's hero Malivert are, as before, concentrated on a female being; and again, as in *Arria Marcella,* this being is a spirit. But an important difference separates Lavinia-Spirite and Arria Marcella: while the latter is attractive chiefly on sensuous grounds, Gautier in no way depicts the former in materialistic terms. Lavinia barely assumes enough density to be perceptible. When Gautier calls attention to her beauty, he emphasizes that it transcends the greatest *mortal* perfection. It is a beauty so transfigured and idealized

3. *Le Conte fantastique en France*, pp. 246–47.

that Malivert easily recognizes Lavinia for what she in fact is, a supernatural being (pp. 65–67).

The milieu in which she is represented to exist is a transcendental region inaccessible to approach through the senses. That it possesses nothing of materiality is suggested by Gautier's imagery in describing it: "Des immensités bleuâtres, où des traînées de lumière creusaient des vallées d'argent et d'or se perdant en perspectives sans bornes, s'ouvraient devant ses yeux fermés; puis ce tableau s'évanouissait pour laisser voir à une profondeur plus grande des ruissellements d'une phosphorescence aveuglante, comme une cascade de soleils liquéfiés qui tomberait de l'éternité dans l'infini; la cascade disparut à son tour, et à sa place s'étendit un ciel de ce blanc intense et lumineux qui revêtit jadis les transfigurés du Thabor. De ce fond, qu'on eût pu croire l'extrême paroxysme de la splendeur, pointaient çà et là des élancements stellaires, des jets plus vifs, des scintillations plus intenses encore" (p. 73).

Lavinia is explicit in qualifying this spirit world as an immaterial region of which the real world is only a veil (pp. 98–99). Its joys cannot therefore be experienced by living beings. Lavinia did not know its pleasures until after her death, when she herself became spirit. In the context of the novel Malivert, too, must die in order to experience fully these same pleasures, which in life he can only dimly intuit. For earthbound man the supernatural existence represented in *Spirite* is thus also a *future* goal. Whereas d'Albert seeks happiness in the present, Octavien in the past, Malivert recognizes that the intangible source of felicity he longs for lies ahead. Knowing that he cannot realize it in life, he gladly accepts the prospect of death, for by dying he will gain happiness everlasting.

While Lavinia does not sum up an ideal as do Madelaine de Maupin and Arria Marcella, she exists in it, and it is by her experience that Gautier defines the pleasures of which the spirit being partakes. She enjoys freedom from all constraints. To move about in the luminous infinity where she resides she has only to will it. She further has experienced brand new perceptions, unknown to earthbound man, which give her full understanding of the peculiarly celestial realities which she beholds. If she is forced to describe these realities in materialistic terms, it is only because, as she explains, language does not have the resources to make them otherwise comprehensible to mortals. Her whole viewpoint is widened. She can see not only the totality of the spirit world but the material universe as well. Everything around her is seen to be infinitely superior to the manifestations of that material reality beyond which the living may not perceive. She hears and understands the music of the spheres in its perfect harmony and is able to comprehend thereby the whole system of the universe, with its structure, its own living thought, and its ultimate aim (pp. 164–68). Indeed, her knowledge is absolute. She understands, by intuition, not only the essence of material things but the idea itself, in its essential state. Experiencing together with this the infinite goodness of the Divinity, she feels only an exhilarating joy (p. 99).

Malivert himself, although still bound to the body, nevertheless catches, by his concentration on Lavinia, glimpses of the pleasures afforded in this extrahuman milieu. His dream of the spirit world presents him with visions of the same luminous, open space which Lavinia already enjoys (pp. 73–74). The love which he anticipates he foresees as eternally satisfying, free from the ravages of time (p. 138). Limitless horizons seem to open to him, and new feelings begin to ferment in his mind, feelings which cannot be satisfactorily communicated, because language is too limited and crude to express them (pp. 187–88).

He experiences, in addition, unknown sensory capabilities. His appreciation of music is enhanced immeasurably (p. 182), and his sense of plastic beauty is so sharpened that he understands for the first time the concepts of proportion and line evident in classical architecture (p. 219). It is clear, however, that this new vision of the old art is of secondary importance in relationship to the transcendental reality which Malivert glimpses. The beauties of nature and of the art of ancient Greece grow pale in comparison with the beauty of Lavinia (pp. 222–23). Indeed, nothing of this world can produce the rapture which he feels at every new revelation permitted him. He feels as if intoxicated (p. 174, et passim), and his only desire is to enhance and perpetuate his ecstasy by gaining the Lost Paradise which Lavinia, as Spirite, holds out to him (p. 186).

The necessary orientation for attaining to the new ideal will be best defined, according to Gautier, as *spiritual.* That Malivert is dissociated from the senses is abundantly evident. When it is a question of material objects, these have no significance for him compared with his desire to settle in the supernatural world. The indifference with which he regards artistic excellence after his introduction to the pleasures of the spirit extends to all objects belonging to the human sphere. His native aloofness from terrestrial involvements, even before he is visited by the ghost of Lavinia, is represented as resulting from a desire to save himself for a higher good than the material world can give him (pp. 45, 59, et passim).

That this desire has been created by Lavinia herself suggests, in addition, that Malivert, as idealist, is not altogether in control of his own destiny (pp. 72, 94, et passim). Lavinia's assertion that she and Malivert are predestined for union in the afterlife further indicates that spirituality is not wholly a matter of will (p. 168). To enjoy the pleasures of the spirit one must be chosen.

Given his distinguished position and the felicity he anticipates, Malivert naturally contributes to the accomplishment of his fate. Convinced that he will indeed enjoy the immaterial pleasures promised by Lavinia, he is single-minded in his quest to hasten the moment of union. Lavinia's admonition that he be intrepid in the face of initial dangers (pp. 98–99) is unnecessary, for his desire to attain to his ideal is irresistible. In his eagerness he draws farther and farther away from society and from whatever objects in the material world once attracted him (pp. 189–90, 214, et passim). He concentrates more and more intently on Lavinia who, in turn, acts in such a way as to draw him ever closer to her (pp. 190–91). While this concentration does indeed give him exhilarating foretastes of pleasures to come, his materiality still prevents actual possession. Full enjoyment, it is emphasized time and time again, demands liberation from one's physical nature (pp. 74, 168, et passim). Malivert will achieve this release in death.

The new conception of the ideal, together with an explicitly negative view of materialism, is already noticeable in *Jettatura* (1856). This short novel belongs as a companion piece with *Spirite* because the ideal has the ethereal quality we have already observed in Lavinia and because it is clear in *Jettatura* that sensuousness must inevitably fail as a means of approaching such an ideal. For Gautier's hero, Paul d'Aspremont, happiness will depend chiefly on pleasures derived through the senses, especially the sense of sight. It is not inappropriate, then, that he is an evil-eye, whose fond look, ironically, is causing the slow deterioration of his fiancée Alicia Ward. When he at last recognizes his pernicious influence, he elects to blind himself rather than lose the opportunity for happiness with Alicia. The surrender of his sight, he comes to understand, will represent in no way a sacrifice. In fact, the statement he makes after putting out his eyes stands as a recognition that true happiness is not necessarily dependent on what one sees: "Je ne regrette rien ... qu'ai-je perdu, en effet? le spectacle monotone des saisons et des jours, la vue des décorations plus ou moins pittoresques où se déroulent les cent actes divers de la triste comédie humaine. —La terre, le ciel, les eaux, les montagnes, les arbres, les fleurs: vaines apparences, redites fastidieuses, formes toujours les mêmes!"[4] This unequivocal rejection of the material world is a far cry from d'Albert's statement of sensuousness cited earlier, which may, for the sake of comparison, be repeated here: "On a beau faire: le bonheur est blanc et rose; on ne peut guère le représenter autrement. Les couleurs tendres lui reviennent de droit. —Il n'a sur sa palette que du vert d'eau, du bleu de ciel et du jaune paille: ses tableaux sont tout dans le clair comme ceux des

4. *Romans et contes* (Paris, 1872), p. 262. Subsequent references to *Jettatura* will be to this edition.

peintres chinois. —Des fleurs, de la lumière, des parfums, une peau soyeuse et douce qui touche la vôtre, une harmonie voilée et qui vient on ne sait d'où, on est parfaitement heureux avec cela; il n'y a pas moyen d'être heureux différemment" (*Maupin*, p. 123). Juxtaposition of these statements separated by twenty years shows the radical change in orientation in Gautier's narratives. D'Aspremont's statement marks a repudiation of the old visual affection, if not of sensuousness altogether.

Yet d'Aspremont loses Alicia anyhow, and the blame must be laid to sensuousness itself. One reason he does not regret losing his sight is that he will still be able to enjoy perceptions through the other senses. He will, moreover, be able to "see" through Alicia's eyes. She will guide him, reporting to him the beauties of the milieux through which they pass (pp. 261–62). He is therefore not so free of his sensuous inclination as we might think. His subjection to the senses is further manifest in his obedience to an impulse to enjoy a last visual orgy before blinding himself: he will go out and allow his eyes to become saturated with the splendid images of nature so that he can see them later in his memory if not in actuality (p. 257). His orgy includes a last fond look at Alicia. This is the look that kills her.

It is significant also that d'Aspremont regards Alicia at all times in materialistic terms. In fact, all of the characters in Gautier's story see her thus. For them her consuming sickness is an unfortunate decline from health. They recall sadly her former strength and grace, like that of an ancient goddess (p. 233). Count Altavilla, recognizing his own materialism, urges d'Aspremont to give up Alicia so that she may regain her *physical* vitality (p. 237).

The reader, however, is led to view Alicia differently. According to *Jettatura* her *essential* nature is otherworldly. Even the materialists in the story recognize her "angelic" quality. D'Aspremont himself calls her "une créature céleste, un ange de Thomas Moore" (p. 196). To her uncle she is like an angel whom God, in His grace, has allowed to walk temporarily among men (p. 222).

Her supposed decline is, in Gautier's terms, actually a gradual spiritualization. Her corporality is already tenuous at the beginning of the story, and it becomes increasingly so. She does not seem to have the crude nature to remain long on earth (p. 222). When d'Aspremont visits her for the last time, he finds her even more ethereal than before: "La beauté si parfaite d'Alicia se spiritualisait par la souffrance: la femme avait presque disparu pour faire place à l'ange; ses chairs étaient transparentes, éthérées, lumineuses; on apercevait l'âme à travers comme une lueur dans une lampe d'albâtre. Ses yeux avaient l'infini du ciel et la scintillation de l'étoile" (p. 258). The final stages of her sickness appear as a sort of vanishing of life, the soul struggling to take its flight back to Heaven: "On eût dit un ange retenu sur terre et ayant la nostalgie du ciel; la beauté d'Alicia était si suave, si délicate, si diaphane, si immatérielle, que la grossière atmosphère humaine ne devait plus être respirable pour elle; on se la figurait planant dans la lumière d'or du Paradis" (p. 265). Her death is to be considered in this context as her soul's resumption of its native otherworldly state. The ideal in *Jettatura* is therefore something transcendental, having nothing of the character of that early ideal symbolized by Madelaine de Maupin. As a transcendental reality, furthermore, it cannot be approached in other than spiritual terms. Sensuousness is without value in seeking the new ideal. In fact it is detrimental. It is because of his unconscious subjection to the senses that d'Aspremont loses contact with his ideal forever. Malivert's success in *Spirite,* on the other hand, is due to his rejection of materialism and to his recognition that to possess the transcendental ideal demands an exclusively spiritual approach.

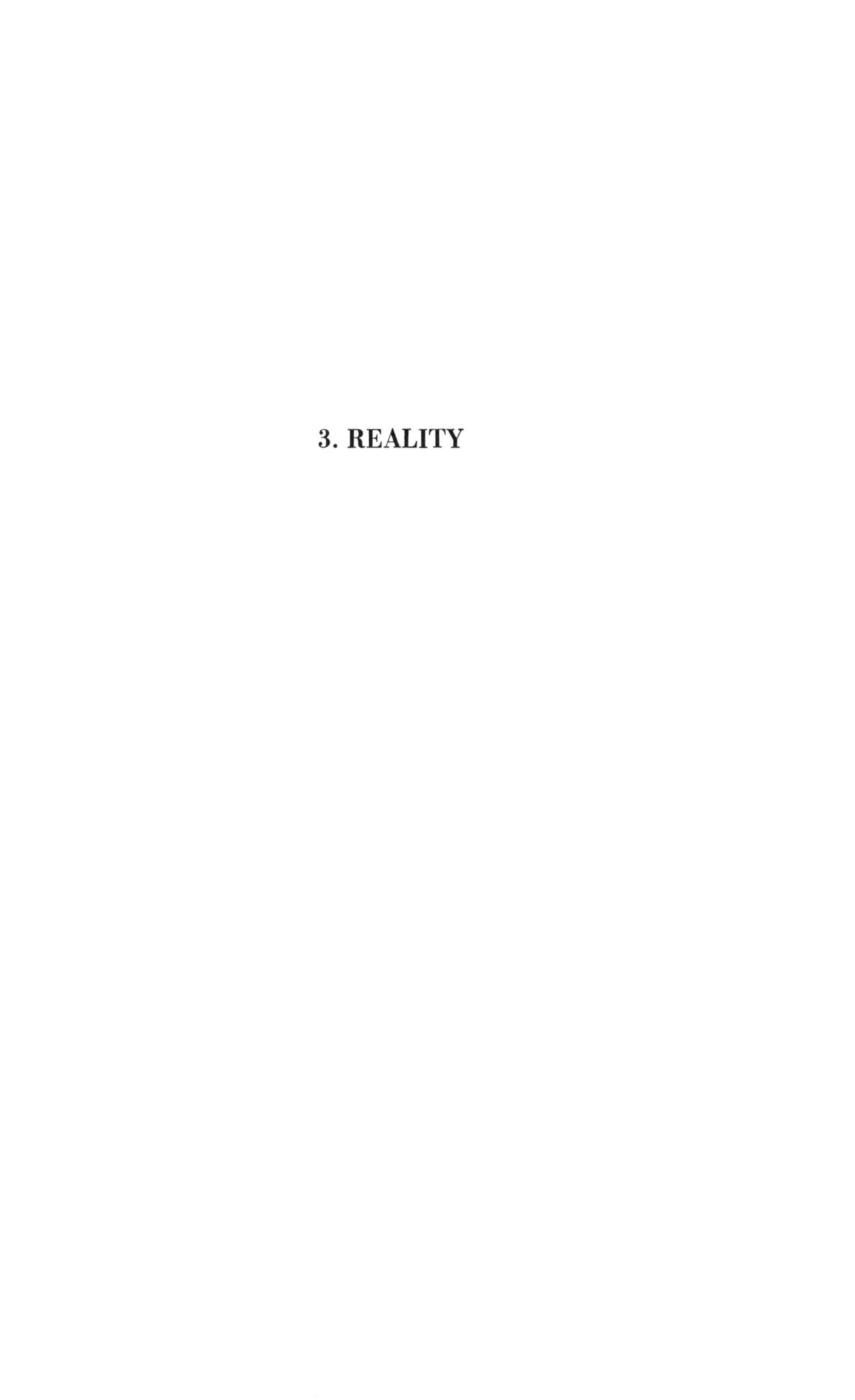

3. REALITY

In the preceding chapters I have alluded to obstacles which pose a threat to the successful quest of the ideal, whatever form it may have. To judge by the attention which they receive, these obstacles are almost as important for the idealist as the ideal which he is pursuing. They do, indeed, show themselves to be closely bound up with his quest, for at every turn the heroes in the narratives find themselves confronted by certain forces or conditions militating against their attainment to or enjoyment of the ideal. What these obstacles are and how Gautier's heroes react to them are therefore questions which demand equal consideration with the ideal. All form a part of the present circumstances in which the idealist finds himself and fall into two general categories: ambient reality and the inner condition of the hero himself.

AMBIENT REALITY

In most of the narratives there is evident a strong antipathy toward the material and ethical aspects of the present context in which Gautier's heroes exist. Modern dress, modern art, modern amusements, the whole modern mentality are represented as unattractive. The superlative male beauty of Fortunio, for example, is diminished by the European fashions he wears in Paris.[1] Modern dress always comes off a poor second in the frequent comparisons Gautier makes between it and the dress of periods in history which he admires. The modern style is barbarous, comparing as unfavorably with the graceful lines of Pompeian robes as would the costume of an American In-

1. *Nouvelles,* 10e éd. (Paris, 1872), p. 26. Subsequent references to *Fortunio* will be to this edition.

dian with the latest Parisian fashions (*CF*, pp. 235–36). As for modern art it no longer possesses the sense of form and proportion which characterizes ancient sculpture. A comment from *Avatar* is representative: "Depuis que le polythéisme a emporté avec lui ces jeunes dieux, ces génies souriants, ces éphèbes célestes aux formes d'une perfection si absolue, d'un rythme si harmonieux, d'un idéal si pur, et que la Grèce antique ne chante plus l'hymne de la beauté en strophes de Paros, l'homme a cruellement abusé de la permission qu'on lui a donnée d'être laid, et, quoique fait à l'image de Dieu, le représente assez mal."[2]

Fortunio cannot find a single modern French sculptor whom he does not consider an unskilled hacker good only for carving pavement stones (*Nouvelles*, p. 125). The motif which introduces *Le Club des hachichins* is the stark contrast between the ugliness of modern buildings and the magnificence of the Hôtel Pimodan, model of an architecture less indifferent than that of the present to beauty and grandeur (*CF*, pp. 189–91).

Modern theaters also come under attack for their foul odors and uncomfortable seats (*CF*, p. 238), while the dancers in a contemporary performance receive even worse abuse: "un essaim de nymphes culottées, sous leurs jupes de gaze, d'un affreux caleçon vert monstre qui les faisait ressembler à des grenouilles piquées de la tarentule" (*CF*, p. 250).

Most aspects of modern life are worthy only of contempt. Pejorative epithets abound in most contexts relating to ambient reality: *barbare, mesquin, prosaïque, laid, affreux, infecte, aride.* The most complete catalogue of the disgusting elements in modern life is made by Fortunio in a letter to a friend in India. Like one of Montesquieu's Persians, except more explicitly, Fortunio inventories and criticizes one by one the components of European culture. The supposed seat of civilization, Europe is far from civilized, according to Fortunio. France, for example, is a pitiful country, its capital a filthy city with a dismal climate. The men and women are un-

2. *Romans et contes* (Paris, 1872), p. 33. Subsequent references to *Avatar* will be to this edition.

attractive, their clothing ugly and their manners coarse. French life offers no luxuries whatsoever. The best restaurants are no more than *gargotes*. The Opera is uncomfortable, its dancers unsightly, and its music dissonant. Indeed, European amusements in general are anything but amusing. France's constitutional monarchy is an incomprehensible form of government. Modern art is undistinguished, nothing of any value having been created in several centuries. Social customs are barbaric. In spite of all this the Europeans are proud of their "accomplishments," thinking that, because they possess newspapers and railroads, they have reached the pinnacle of culture. Fortunio rejects even France's most charming courtesan because of her "stupides idées européennes." Unable to tolerate for very long the state of modern Western "civilization," he gladly departs for his home in the Orient (*Nouvelles*, pp. 153–57).

Most of the stories represent explicitly the contrast between ordinary life and the milieu considered to be ideal. Romuald's existence as a priest is drab and sterile compared with the magnificent dream life he leads with Clarimonde (*CF*, pp. 93, 109–10). The return from the dream state to real life is always accompanied by deep melancholy. The hero of *La Cafetière* recognizes on awakening that he will never again be happy (*CF*, p. 21). Likewise Octavien finishes out his life in profound sadness after losing contact with Arria Marcella (*CF*, pp. 250–51).

Gautier also expresses the antithesis between the ideal and present reality through contrasts between ordinary women and the heroines who symbolize the ideal. No one can satisfy d'Albert's preconception of beauty. Even his attachment to the most beautiful and charming woman in his society, Rosette, fails to give him the supreme pleasure he demands. On his return from Pompeii, Octavien marries a beautiful English girl and frequents a society distinguished by its charming women, but neither his wife nor others can break the spell which the memory of Arria Marcella holds over him.

The meanness of modern life is further evident in a number

of instances where the contemporary era is represented as a degeneration from an earlier Golden Age. This Golden Age may be viewed primarily in artistic terms, as in *Fortunio,* where the hero himself stands as the last example of superlative male beauty gone from the world since the advent of Christianity (*Nouvelles,* p. 124). Or the concept of the Golden Age may represent the mentality of a whole culture. The Hôtel Pimodan in *Le Club des hachichins* is a last vestige of the seventeenth-century penchant for grandeur. The narrator, in his modern dress, feels himself to be a stain upon this magnificent environment (*CF,* pp. 190–91). The present epoch seems all the more contemptible as it is set next to the attractiveness of past ages.

What is most disturbing for Gautier's heroes is the very real threat ambient reality poses to success in quest of the ideal. Forces from real life may attempt to thwart the idealist. In *La Morte amoureuse,* even before Romuald begins to dream his vivid dreams of life with Clarimonde, Father Sérapion warns him against her and urges him to greater concentration on his priestly duties (*CF,* pp. 89, 101–2). Mme d'Ymbercourt of *Spirite* symbolizes reality at pains to distract the hero from his goal (*Spirite,* p. 29). The Baron de Féroë warns Malivert against the dangers of earthly involvements: "Ne vous engagez dans aucun lien terrestre. Restez libre pour l'amour, qui peut-être va vous visiter. Les esprits ont l'œil sur vous, et vous pourriez vous repentir éternellement dans l'extramonde d'une faute commise dans celui-ci" (*Spirite,* p. 28). Throughout *Spirite* there are suggestions that the idealist must be actively concerned to keep his soul free, lest the material world gain control over his life.

On the other hand, enjoyment of the ideal may be disrupted by some representative of ambient reality. In *Omphale,* an uncle intrudes upon his nephew's pleasure by removing a tapestry, one of whose female figures the nephew dreams is initiating him to the delights of erotic love (*CF,* pp. 74–75). Father Sérapion's role in *La Morte amoureuse* is analogous to that of the uncle. Sérapion's campaign to rescue Romuald from worldliness finally succeeds when he manages to exhume Clarimonde's body and destroy the vampire residing there. Other intrusions from the outside may be less sensational, but the idealists' reactions are the same: antipathy toward the intruder, and lifelong sadness at the loss of contact with the ideal.

Sérapion is the representative of a force in ambient reality which, by the elaborateness of its representation, stands out as the most dangerous threat to the idealist: Christianity. What is offensive is the Christian mentality, and hostility to it is evident in the earliest narratives. While d'Albert admires the materialism which reveres Venus, he despises Christianity —symbolized in the Virgin Mary—for its mystical, otherworldly bent as well as for its gloomy animosity toward the pleasures of this life (*Maupin*, pp. 190–94).

Christianity is hateful chiefly because of its puritanism, which derives directly from this essentially ascetic outlook. Antagonistic to matter, to beauty, and to form, the Christian mind will go to any length to counteract materialistic inclinations. It is Romuald's attraction to physical pleasures that shocks Father Sérapion into action. Sérapion views Clarimonde as the devil incarnate, and he cannot rest until he has saved Romuald from the perdition toward which he sees him rushing headlong. Sérapion's actions, ending with his brutal destruction of the personification of beauty, youth, and life, reflects the workings of the puritanical mind which, taking its delights in contemplation of the afterlife, has only contempt for the present. Intolerant of anyone who seeks pleasure through the senses, the puritan considers it his primary task to act as Sérapion does, forcing everyone into his own tight moral frame.

The same outlook is also evident in *Arria Marcella*. Arrius Diomèdes, the heroine's father, appears as grim and austere, his face lined by the suffering he has undergone through frequent self-mortification. He roundly condemns his daughter's life-loving paganism, and calls on her to disavow the demons which she calls her gods. Unable to tolerate her refusal to bend to what she terms his morose religion, he cries out an exorcistic formula which destroys her (*CF*, pp. 247–49).

Nor have Christian asceticism and puritanism mitigated with time. The attitude which characterizes Father Sérapion and Arrius Diomèdes not only shows itself in the modern world but, worst of all, prevails. It is even visible in the material sphere. According to the narratives, much of the ugliness in the modern world is ultimately attributable to Christianity. The prevalence of asceticism in the modern mentality is particularly galling. D'Albert frets that Christianity did not die with the early Christians but has continued to exert its stifling influence up to the present. According to him, modern man views the world through Christ's shroud. The three words with which he characterizes Christianity—virginity, mysticism, and melancholy—all diametrically opposed to his own enthusiasm for sensuous pleasures—he qualifies as three moral sicknesses epidemic in modern times (*Maupin*, p. 194). In *Arria Marcella* antipathy to Christianity is even more intense. That the Christian outlook still infects the modern mind is evident in the contrast between the pagan *Voie des Tombeaux* and Christian cemeteries. While the former are bright places where even the tombs bear witness to a love of life, the latter are lugubrious sites creating only gloomy thoughts of death in the mind of the visitor (*CF*, pp. 221–22). That these are, moreover, cemeteries built by modern men suggests again that asceticism is most surely to be considered a disease still virulent. The idealist, therefore, has much to fear from Christianity. As Arrius Diomèdes disrupts Octavien's pleasure, so the puritanical mentality may subvert the modern idealist's pursuit of happiness.

Another outside force creating a threat to the successful quest of the ideal is time, which, by its inevitable passage, has the potential for preventing contact with or lasting possession of the ideal. In the narratives we find both direct and indirect statements of concern regarding the passage of time. In *Omphale*, for instance, the narrator expresses regret at the deterioration of past artistic beauty and at the loss of charming old customs (*CF*, pp. 65–66, 68–69). In *Spirite* Malivert notes sadly the irrevocability of time, which prevents our reliving past moments in order to rectify old wrongs (p. 137). One of the delights he foresees in the spiritual orientation is escape from natural subjection to time. Whereas for the materialist time quickly erodes the physical charms which first spark earthly love, for the man spiritually oriented it no longer poses a threat (p. 138).

A major pleasure experienced by Gautier's heroes in the dream state is escape from time. Time seems actually to go off its track, so that the hero suddenly awakens in another age (*Arria Marcella, CF*, p. 241). The narrator of *Le Pied de momie* experiences a journey back in time to the days of the Pharaohs (*CF*, pp. 159–60). The hero of *Le Roman de la momie* has the sensation, while exploring an Egyptian burial crypt, that he has in fact returned to Egypt as it was thirty-five centuries ago (pp. 173–74). Upsets occurring in the normal sequence of time thus give the hero an opportunity to make apparently live contact with the near or distant past. These narratives end, however, with time victorious over the idealist. The narrator of *La Cafetière,* for example, desires the ineffable joy which he experiences in his dream to last forever. But in the context of the narrative dawn comes and his dream vision vanishes. Octavien, on awakening from his dream, attempts to re-establish contact with Pompeii, but in vain. The past for him is lost forever.

In the narratives having to do with ancient Egypt the importance of time is clarified. We have already observed that one of the admirable aspects of the Egyptian mentality was its dream of permanence (*Pied de momie, CF*, pp. 151, 161; *Roman de la momie,* pp. 164, 184). Both stories emphasize a relationship which exists between permanence and art (*Pied de momie, CF*, p. 159; *Roman de la momie,* loc. cit.). For the ancient Egyptians the primary function of craftsmanship was to serve the desire for eternity. According to Evandale, the Egyptians were combating the passage of the body into a void. For them time brought a cessation of life, a fact impossible to accept. By their embalming techniques they thus sought to counteract the dissolution of the body after death. By art the body would be preserved and, in a sense, continue to live. Evandale's sympathy with Egyptian religious practices thus coincides with an attitude we associate with the early and middle narratives: enthusiasm for life. For a man in love with living, time can represent only a source of anguish.

Antipathy toward the passage of time is implicit in other works. In *Arria Marcella* the narrator expresses his faith that nothing dies, but lives on forever as spirit (*CF*, p. 245). Lavinia, of *Spirite,* actually fulfills this belief; she is a spirit existing eternally in a supernatural world. For Malivert a major benefit deriving from the spiritual orientation is the fact that time loses its power. While earlier attempts to conquer time fail because the heroes' outlook is too materialistic and the ideal itself too tangible to be free of temporal contingency, Malivert suffers in no way from temporality. Through his concentration on suprasensual realities he escapes the threat of time.

The Inner Threat

Although ambient mentality and time appear as threats to the idealist's quest during the whole period covered by Gautier's narratives, their importance in the later stories gives way before threats far more subtle and difficult to combat because they originate in the seeker's own being. These, too, recur from an early date, but, compared with those from outside, they become paramount for Gautier's heroes only in the works of the 1850's.

The most important is the threat of the personal flaw. Several failures by heroes to make contact with or to hold on to their ideal result in large part from defective concentration. Romuald's case is representative. It is a plain conflict of interests: his desire to enjoy worldly pleasures is opposed by his desire for salvation. He might even be said to have two contradictory ideals, if the latter were viewed more affirmatively. But Romuald's desire to save his soul results more from the fear of hell than from an enthusiastic zeal to enjoy Heavenly bliss. Nevertheless, the question of salvation poses itself so vigorously that it prevents single-minded concentration on the desired ideal. In the terms of Gautier's story Romuald's situation is untenable. He cannot long remain torn between two equally strong forces. Nor can he give up one or the other without coming to grief. The question of wherein lies the least suffering is unanswerable. When he at last does capitulate to his religious fear, he wins only lifelong heartbreak for having at the same time renounced a fundamental source of happiness.

In *Jettatura* Gautier presents a more complex case. D'Aspremont's problem is analogous to that of Romuald, except that d'Aspremont is not fully conscious of his conflict of interests. His case is one of misunderstanding in regard to the kind of approach necessary for the particular ideal in question. We observed in the preceding chapter that in *Jettatura* the ideal is essentially immaterial and transcendent. We also saw that d'Aspremont fails to consider that ideal in the terms proper to it because he approaches it materialistically. Recognizing that d'Aspremont is a man instinctively bound to the senses, we are led to view not only his sight but his whole orientation as "evil," since it is precisely his materialism that prevents union with the ideal. Imperfect concentration here is the result of ignorance.

Avatar brings us to further consideration of the personality and its relationship to the ideal. Gautier's hero, Octave de Saville, is represented as having some defect in his character which prevents his coming even close to his goal. What this defect is, is not clear; Saville simply does not have the necessary qualities to allow him to realize his desires. *Avatar* is the story of his attempt to side-step the issue by changing his identity in order to possess the woman who symbolizes his ideal. Appropriating her husband's physical form fails, however, for she recognizes Saville's character and rebuffs him. Understanding that his action was misguided, Saville attempts to resume his identity but dies in the attempt. That he simply does not possess the nature proper for enjoyment of the ideal is evident in the epitaph which Gautier assigns him: "Ame obscurément sublime, il ne savait qu'aimer et mourir" (*Romans et contes*, p. 126).

The lessons to be inferred from these representations of failure through personal flaw are clear. The personal flaw is a real threat to the idealist's pursuit. If he is not, first and foremost, single-minded, he can never expect success. But single-mindedness is insufficient to ensure lasting union with the ideal. Paul d'Aspremont and Octave de Saville fail for other reasons. In *Jettatura* Gautier suggests that a particular ideal demands an orientation proper to it. D'Aspremont's materialistic approach is inappropriate, given the transcendental character of the ideal. In *Avatar* Saville fails because of something more fundamental: the fact that he simply does not have it in himself to possess the ideal. And there is *no* way he can acquire the necessary qualities. One is what one is. The imperfect idealist can only regretfully reconcile himself to the impossibility of capturing his ideal.

Spirite bears out these lessons. Malivert achieves union with his ideal precisely because he is naturally endowed with the qualities proper for union with a transcendental reality (pp. 111–12). Indeed, he is doubly blessed, actually being predestined to enjoy the pleasures of the spirit world (pp. 168–69). According to the Baron de Féroë, Malivert has only to submit to the force guiding him and he will as if automatically attain to his ideal (p. 175). In addition, the spiritual orientation—which, incidentally, proceeds directly from his character—corresponds perfectly to the ideal he seeks. His single-mindedness goes without saying, and together with his natural endowments and appropriate orientation, it ensures him of success. Thus the naturally spiritual-minded idealist will not have to *strive* to possess his ideal; he will attain to it as a matter of course.

Another personal problem is a failing of men in general: the inability of the human body and mind to tolerate prolonged pleasure. This inner threat is evident throughout the period covered by the narratives. Gautier seems to have recognized, very early, man's weak constitution in relationship to intense pleasures, for already in *Mademoiselle de Maupin* d'Albert calls attention to it. Recalling a particularly exciting moment of love with Rosette, he says: "C'est peut-être la seule fois de ma vie que je n'ai pas été désappointé, et que la réalité m'a paru aussi belle que l'idéal .... Mais, en vérité, je ne crois pas qu'un homme de chair pût résister une heure à des voluptés si pénétrantes; deux baisers comme cela pomperaient une existence entière, et feraient vide complet dans une âme et dans un corps" (p. 102). The narrator of *Le Club des hachichins* is already at the point of generalizing on this conviction. Under the influence of the drug he experiences the most intense delights, which he later evaluates thus: "L'enveloppe humaine, *qui a si peu de force pour le plaisir* ... n'aurait pu supporter une plus haute pression de bonheur" (*CF*, p. 203; italics mine). Gautier returns to the same notion as late as 1865, in *Spirite,* where Lavinia calls Malivert back from a seizure of ecstasy brought on by his introduction to the transcendental reality: "le génie est vraiment divin, il invente l'idéal, il entrevoit la beauté supérieure et l'éternelle lumière. Où ne monte-t-il pas lorsqu'il a pour ailes la foi et l'amour! Mais redescendez, revenez aux régions où l'air est respirable pour les poumons mortels .... Craignez la folie, l'extase y touche. Calmez-vous et si vous m'aimez, vivez encore de la vie humaine" (p. 189).

Closely related to man's inability to tolerate prolonged pleasure is his tendency to satiety with even the most exquisite delights. In *Spirite* the narrator calls particular attention to the boredom which seems naturally to attend earthly liaisons (p. 138). This weakness is a major factor in the outcome of *Mademoiselle de Maupin*: the very reason why Madelaine leaves d'Albert after only one night of love. In a farewell letter to him she explains that, although their night together was consummately pleasurable and might even be followed by others equally delightful, d'Albert would sooner or later become tired of her, and his intense passion would ultimately dwindle into indifference. Or she might become tired of him. Unable to bear the thought of such a deterioration of love, she has decided to disappear, preferring to leave d'Albert with a happy memory rather than with an undesirable presence (pp. 370–71).

Essentially the same point is discernible in the vampire motif in *La Morte amoureuse.* Clarimonde, as we have seen, is the symbol of total sensual pleasure. She is also a vampire who requires Romuald's blood to stay alive. We are led to understand that the intense enjoyment of such total delight as life with her provides may ultimately be harmful to the sensualist. His body simply may not be strong enough to tolerate his bliss. The main point, however, is evident in the young priest's reaction to the knowledge that his beloved will destroy him. He is willing—even eager—to give his blood if it means he may continue to enjoy her: "la femme me répondait du vampire .... Je me serais ouvert le bras moi-même et je lui aurais dit: Bois! et que mon amour s'infiltre dans ton corps avec mon sang!" (*CF,* p. 113). D'Albert says almost the same thing: although he recognizes that the result of intense pleasure may very well be untimely death, he is willing to accept that result to have an hour of the ecstasy he desires (*Maupin,* p. 102). That Gautier's heroes thus choose to risk death to attain to their ideal reflects the intensity of their desires. A less committed idealist would stop short of death.

This extreme enthusiasm regarding materialism diminishes, however. The attitude implicit in *Le Club des hachichins,* for example, is one of pessimism; for what happens to the narrator under the influence of the drug symbolizes the fate of one who seeks happiness exclusively through the senses. While the narrator enjoys supreme delight in the early moments of his hallucination, the final stage is a veritable nightmare. He becomes bogged down, as it were, in materiality. Evil forces attempt to imprison him for eternity. A Hoffmannesque figure steals his brain (*CF,* pp. 205–10). This brief hallucinatory experience may be considered a microcosm of the real sense-oriented quest. Not only can a man not long stand the intense pleasures of sense stimulation, but enjoyment itself gives way to pain and suffering the farther one goes in pursuit of a tangible good.

Materiality may also cripple from within. Whereas *Le Club des hachichins* shows the idealist caught and as if frozen in *exterior* materiality, the careers of other heroes suggest that one's own corporality also poses a threat. Man's very physical nature prevents full enjoyment not only in terms of the senses but also in terms of the spiritual orientation. This conviction may explain the function of the dream motif in a number of the narratives. In every representation of a dream experience the hero finds liberation from his own corporality that allows him broader perceptions, thus richer enjoyment. In as early a work as *La Cafetière,* the narrator dreams pleasures unknown to him in the waking state. Freed, as he says, from his "prison de boue," he experiences a new order of reality. He meets the most beautiful woman he has ever seen. His new emotions are exhilarating in the extreme. His pleasure is greater than any he has ever known. Achieving perfect communication and understanding with the woman of his dream, he desires only to remain in this state forever (*CF*, pp. 16–19). Upon his necessary return to reality, he recognizes that ordinary existence, with its built-in physical strictures, will be henceforth unbearably sad (*CF*, p. 21).

In *Arria Marcella* the threat of human materiality is implicit but nevertheless present. Octavien achieves contact with his retrospective ideal only in dream—and only once. On reawakening to ordinary reality, he is left prey, like the narrator of *La Cafetière,* to an ineradicable melancholy (*CF*, p. 250). Nor does his conscious attempt to restore contact with ancient Pompeii succeed. The barrier built into physical existence cannot be crossed.

The same function may also belong to the use of hallucinogens. In both *La Pipe d'opium* and *Le Club des hachichins* the narrator calls particular attention to his feeling of liberation, under the effect of the drugs, from the oppressive sense of his own materiality. Unhampered, he gains access to new, unknown perceptions and capabilities. In the later account he also experiences a delightful sensation of euphoria: "J'étais dans cette période bienheureuse du hachich que les Orientaux appellent le *kief*. Je ne sentais plus mon corps; les liens de la matière et de l'esprit étaient déliés; je me mouvais par ma seule volonté dans un milieu qui n'offrait pas de résistance" (*CF*, p. 204).

But again, as in *La Cafetière* and *Arria Marcella,* the narrator's own corporality ultimately supersedes the dream. Neither opium nor hashish can provide enduring sensuous delights. Their effect wears off, the narrator wakes up, and the novelties of the hallucination are lost. In *Le Club des hachichins,* as we have seen, materiality overtakes the narrator in the very midst of his hallucination. A while ago, we observed that it was the reality surrounding him in which he seemed to become caught. In addition he has the exasperating sensation that his own feet turn to marble as he attempts to escape the nightmare which his hallucination has become (*CF*, p. 208). Not only may outside objects in time stifle the idealist but also his own physical nature *will* ultimately regain domination over its victim.

4. SUMMARY AND CONCLUSION

Study of Gautier's narratives shows that the character of the ideal which his heroes posit as a potential source of happiness changes gradually but radically from the early to the later works. The evolution which takes place is visible in the heroines, who either symbolize a given ideal or, as in the case of Lavinia, reside in the ideal milieu and thus are able to describe its pleasures. The early ideal, summed up in Madelaine de Maupin, is conceived as the material embodiment of essential beauty. It is thus an *object,* enjoyment of which is sought in the present. Although d'Albert finds his ideal realized, *Mademoiselle de Maupin* cannot, for all that, be read as a success story. The supreme happiness which d'Albert enjoys with Madelaine is short-lived, for she disappears after a single night of love, explaining that she could not tolerate the inevitable deterioration of his passion. If we are consistent in interpreting Gautier's novel, we are forced to read Madelaine's statement as an assertion that material beauty cannot provide lasting happiness, not because of some flaw in itself but because of a psychological defect in the beholder.

Arria Marcella is the symbol of another ideal, at once cultural and historical. What she stands for is the ethos of paganism. *Arria Marcella,* as well as *Le Roman de la momie,* thus represents the quest of happiness in the mental re-creation of attractive moments from history. Here, too, the search ends in failure. Octavien's imagination is not strong enough to restore contact with the past once it is broken. Evandale cannot even make the proper contact. Again, although other factors come into play, the fault lies, in part at least, with the idealist himself.

In *Spirite* the ideal is transcendental, completely outside the world of sense. It not only has no relationship to material reality; it is, in fact, antagonistic toward it. Also contrary to the other ideals, the new one abundantly fulfills its promise of extreme and enduring ecstasy which Gautier's hero—like all those before him—longs to experience. *Spirite* is the one significant story of success among all the narratives. As such, its ideal appears in retrospect to the reader as the only one worthy of serious pursuit.

The narratives also represent shifts in orientation toward the respective ideals. The material ideal is accompanied by a sensuous affection in the idealist. Happiness is sought through broad satisfaction of the senses. D'Albert's approach is, as we have observed, close to an esthetic outlook. But *esthetic* is too limited an adjective to define properly his way of viewing the world. To gain the satisfaction he demands, all of his senses must come into play, not only the visual and the tactile. This is not a case of crude sensualism. In *Mademoiselle de Maupin* there is a sharp distinction between the gratification of carnal desire and the loftier pleasure sought by d'Albert. The sensualist is easily satisfied: "Le sensuel va chez les courtisanes chercher de faciles amours, ou des raffinements impudiques; une joue fardée, une jupe courte, une gorge débraillée, un propos libertin, il est heureux; son œil blanchit, sa lèvre se trempe; il atteint au dernier degré de son bonheur, il a l'extase de sa grossière volupté" (p. 63). The difference between this kind of crude desire and d'Albert's idealism is recognized by Madelaine: "ce qui me plaît en lui, c'est qu'il ne cherche pas à s'assouvir brutalement comme les autres hommes; il a une perpétuelle aspiration et un souffle toujours soutenu vers le beau, —vers le beau matériel seulement, il est vrai, mais c'est encore un noble penchant, et qui suffit à le maintenir dans les pures régions" (p. 356).

The character of the orientation in the stories of the middle stage is ambiguous. Octavien still displays a materialistic disposition—his interest in ancient art, for example, betrays a proclivity to what touches the senses—but the esthetic-sensuous bent is no longer exclusive. Not only is Octavien interested in a whole culture, but history as a source of pleasure denies, by its very nature, the possibility of a totally sensuous orientation. The past is, like Arria Marcella, a spirit. It can never be fully reincarnated but must, by definition, be enjoyed in the mind.

Recourse to nonmaterialistic means for achieving happiness takes on even greater importance in *Spirite*. Malivert's attitude is, in fact, the very antithesis of the early materialism. He recognizes that the senses have no place in the pursuit of the transcendental ideal. What is demanded is an exclusively spiritual orientation. Nor is this approach felt to be burdensome. Malivert is glad to give up whatever slight interest he may have in the world around him. While he may enjoy a new appreciation of art—one which, incidentally, is a by-product of his spiritual outlook—the appeal of all objects from the material world is as nothing compared with the attraction he feels toward transcendental realities. His successful quest of these realities underscores again the failure of materialism and shows the promise of spirituality.

That the question of present reality has almost equal importance with the search for an ideal is evidenced by the large place which considerations of reality occupy in Gautier's narratives. Indeed, this problem is but the other side of the coin: as the idealist seeks a source of true and lasting happiness, he repeatedly encounters forces and circumstances in his present situation which militate against a successful quest. In most cases these raise an insurmountable barrier between him and his ideal, so that his quest ends in failure.

Forces from the outside play a major role in thwarting the idealists of the earlier narratives. Moralistic meddlers intrude. Time is irrevocable. In the narratives of the 1850's the threat of personal imperfection comes to predominate. Both *Jettatura* and *Avatar* stress the influence of inner flaws on the quest of the ideal.

While the immediate causes of failure may differ from story to story, the fundamental reason is always the same, if implicit: lack of freedom. If d'Albert were not subject to the human drift toward satiety, he would be able to enjoy prolonged possession of his ideal. If asceticism were not prevalent —and intrusive—Octavien would be able to find lasting pleasure in the ideal he seeks in the past. If the prevailing morality and his own lack of single-mindedness had not been present, Romuald would not have to live out his life in regret. Without absolute freedom, happiness, according to the narratives, is impossible; and, given the nature of ambient reality and of man himself, freedom is not to be had. In this regard all the narratives but *Spirite* are plaintive variations on a common Romantic theme: the overwhelming power of circumstances and the inability of the idealist to escape them.

In *Spirite* all of these obstacles are reintroduced and overcome. Freedom shows itself to be essential here, too. The idealist succeeds in his quest of the transcendental ideal in large part because he is liberated from all those forces which barred the way of his predecessors.

Least important at this late date are whatever threats may be created by outside reality. Malivert has, by his own word (p. 59), always been suspicious of material involvements. His refusal to form earthly attachments is the result of his rejection of the ambience in which he exists as being empty of the kind of satisfactions he demands. After his introduction to the extrahuman reality he becomes even more antipathetic to the world around him, finally breaking with it altogether. The rupture is general, too, taking in not only representatives of an unattractive society but any object which might appeal to the senses of one less spiritually oriented.

Malivert also gains release from his human subjection to time. Time in the narratives is chiefly important as a function of materialism: it constitutes a threat because sooner or later it destroys all objects of pleasure and finally swallows up the idealist himself. With his interest in the transcendental ideal Malivert has nothing of that depressing sense of relentless movement toward the void to which Gautier alludes in *Le Roman de la momie*. For the man turned toward *intangible* sources of pleasure the ravages of time have no significance.

Finally, Malivert achieves liberation from the obstacle of materiality. The question of the idealist's own physical nature receives particularly elaborate treatment in *Spirite*. When, in a dream, Malivert has the opportunity to behold a reflection of the transcendental reality in all its splendor, the narrator explains that in sleep the soul is free enough of its corporal bonds to glimpse the spirit world. But the dreaming idealist catches only a glimpse, for man in sleep still has a tie, tenuous but sure, to materiality. Actual settlement in the extramaterial world is possible only for souls absolutely free (p. 74). When Lavinia describes her otherworldly existence to Malivert, she emphasizes that he will not be able to enjoy its pleasures in his present state, because his human materiality prevents his bridging the gap separating the real world from the transcendental (pp. 168, 170). The same problem obtains in the realm of art. The composer of genius, Lavinia says, may well conceive an ideal, but his *human infirmity,* his materiality, necessarily prevents his attaining to it (p. 182). Lavinia, however, is able to complete the master's work, rendering perfectly the essential note that the living creator could not achieve. It is freedom from her physical nature that gives her this power. That Malivert must, as she did, pass through death to reach his ideal means that attainment to the transcendental good demands total rejection of the body as well as of attraction to tangible goods outside. This, accompanied by a reorientation toward the spirit, ensures the idealist of happiness.

It would appear easy to find justifications for seeing Gautier's narratives as chapters of a psychic autobiography. That he returned fairly regularly to the subject of the ideal over a period of thirty-five years might imply an obsessive preoccupation in Gautier himself. Especially the relatively neat evolution which his heroes follow might suggest that Gautier was dramatizing in his narratives his own experiences in search of happiness.

His apparent intrusions into certain stories also might suggest that a coincidence exists between his thought and the attitudes embodied in his heroes. To see such a parallel would seem natural particularly for instances where a narrator comments disparagingly on ambient reality. Gautier's antipathy toward his age is well known.[1] Recognizing how he actually felt toward contemporary society, we might accept other attitudes present in the narratives as expressions of his personal feelings.

Scholarly precedent, too, might invite us to judge the man by his work. It is common in Gautier criticism to use his works as bases on which to reconstruct what are inferred to be aspects of his thought.[2]

This is not possible, however, at least in the case of the ideal, for there is not enough evidence to confirm that Gautier was recounting in his stories his own pursuit of happiness. He is acknowledged to have been extremely reticent about publicizing his inner life,[3] and insofar as a possible quest of happiness is concerned, he is indeed uncommunicative. Even if documents exist, they are inaccessible. Until we have uncovered explicit statements by Gautier on this aspect of his biography, we shall have to withhold judgment.

This in no way means that the narratives of the ideal are without value. Understanding them compels us to change the

1. Certain critical writings on the contemporary theater repeat almost verbatim such hostile assessments as those introduced in *Fortunio* and *Arria Marcella*. See, for pertinent citations, Richardson, *Théophile Gautier,* pp. 60, 61–62, 64, et passim. Gautier's contempt for modern middle-class values, so evident in the narratives, shows also in the preface to *Mademoiselle de Maupin* (ed. Boschot, pp. 2, 25, 28–31) and in the little accessible correspondence. See, for example, his letter to Nerval in Gérard de Nerval, *Œuvres,* eds. Albert Béguin et Jean Richer (Paris, 1952–61), I, 804.

2. See, for example, Paul Bernard, "Théophile Gautier," *Etudes* (1912), I, 328; Adolphe Boschot, Introduction à *Mademoiselle de Maupin,* p. xxxi; Castex, *Le Conte fantastique en France,* pp. 215, 246–47, et passim; Jasinski, *Les Années romantiques de Th. Gautier,* p. 327, et passim; Schneider, *La Littérature fantastique en France,* pp. 215–21; Poulet, *Etudes sur le temps humain,* pp. 278–307; George, *Short Fiction in France, 1800–1850,* p. 188.

3. Bourget, *Pages de critique et de doctrine,* I, 67–68, 82; Castex, *Le Conte fantastique en France,* p. 247.

notion usually held of Gautier's literary character. Gautier is not only the critic, the votary of beauty, the verbal artist, and the objectivist. The stories which have been considered in this essay make clear that his work also has its profoundly human aspect. The questions which the narratives pose reveal a Gautier sensitive to a number of fundamental issues. What is the potential of the imagination? What are its limits? What is the relationship between the individual and time? What are the ingredients of freedom? Above all, how can a man find perfect happiness? The answers which emerge from the stories situate Gautier in a long tradition. The careers of his heroes say what numbers of thinkers have said since the beginnings of recorded thought, that the solutions to man's deepest problems lie not in the world but in the way of the spirit.

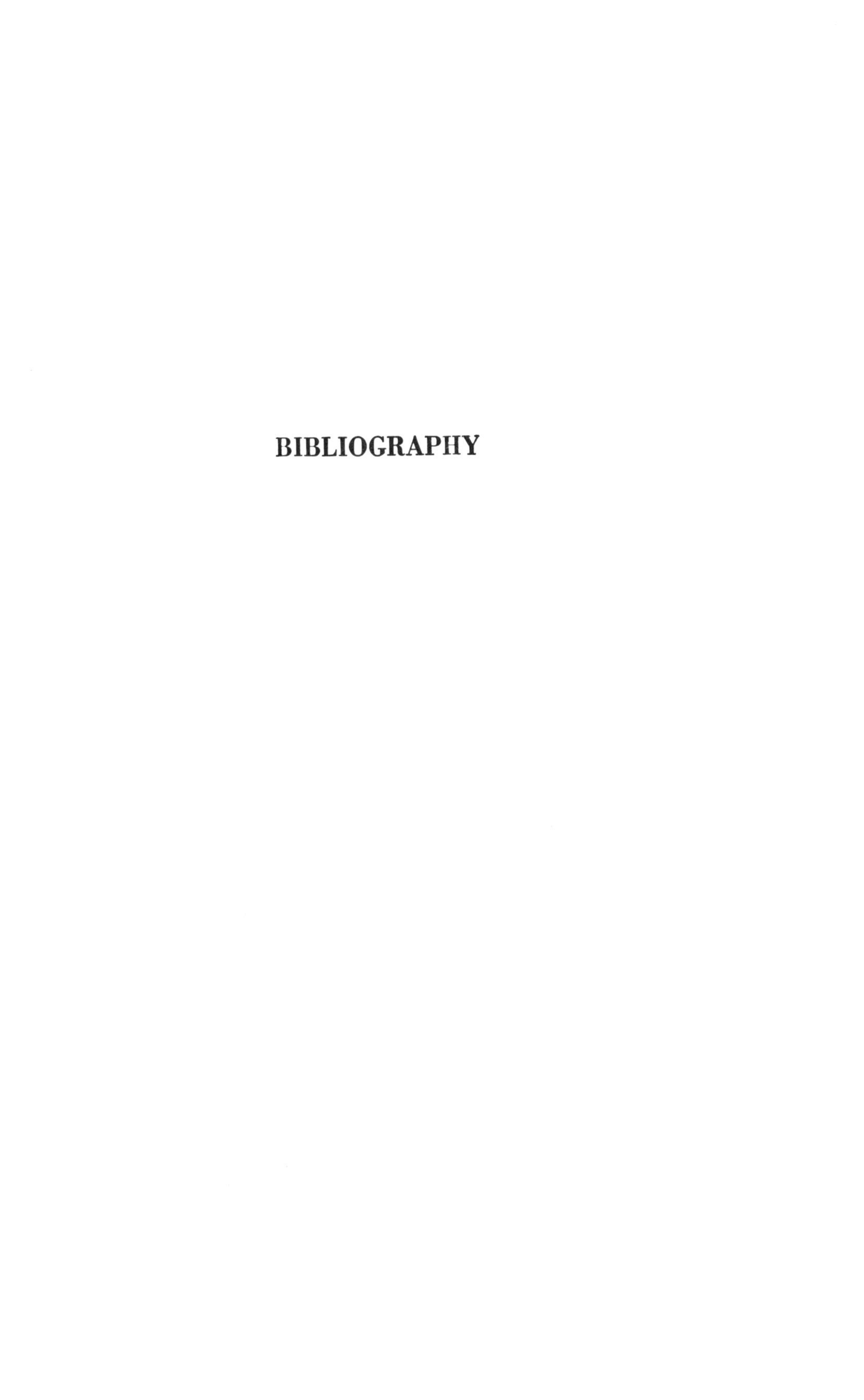

BIBLIOGRAPHY

EDITIONS OF GAUTIER'S NARRATIVES

Contes fantastiques. Paris, 1962. Includes: *La Cafetière, Onuphrius, Omphale, La Morte amoureuse, La Pipe d'opium, Le Chevalier double, Le Pied de momie, Deux acteurs pour un rôle, Une Visite nocturne, Le Club des hachichins, Arria Marcella.*

Mademoiselle de Maupin, ed. Adolphe Boschot. Nouvelle éd. Paris [1955].

Nouvelles, 10e éd. Paris, 1872. Includes: *Fortunio, La Toison d'or, Omphale, Le Petit Chien de la marquise, Le Nid de rossignols, La Morte amoureuse, La Châine d'or, ou l'amant partagé, Une Nuit de Cléopâtre, Le Roi Candaule.*

Le Roman de la momie, précédé de trois contes antiques: *Une Nuit de Cléopâtre, Le Roi Candaule, Arria Marcella,* ed. Adolphe Boschot. Paris, 1963.

Romans et contes. Paris, 1872. Includes: *Avatar, Jettatura, Arria Marcella, La Mille et deuxième nuit, Le Pavillon sur l'eau, L'Enfant aux souliers de pain, Le Chevalier double, Le Pied de momie, La Pipe d'opium, Le Club des hachichins.*

Spirite, 3e éd. Paris, 1872.

WORKS CONSULTED

Antoine-Orliac. "Essai sur le pessimisme chez les Parnassiens," *MdF,* CCVI (1928), 5–19.

Baudelaire, Charles. *Œuvres,* ed. Y.-G. Le Dantec. Paris, 1954.

Bernard, Paul. "Théophile Gautier," *Etudes* (1912), I, 313–36, 644–65; II, 627–53.

Boschot, Adolphe. *Théophile Gautier.* Paris, 1933.

Bourget, Paul. *Pages de critique et de doctrine.* 2 vols. Paris, 1912.

Caillois, Roger, ed. *Anthologie du fantastique.* 2 vols. Paris, 1966.

———, ed. *Fantastique: soixante récits de terreur.* Paris, 1958.

Castex, Pierre-Georges. *Le Conte fantastique en France de Nodier à Maupassant.* Paris, 1951.

Dillingham, Louise B. *The Creative Imagination of Théophile Gautier: A Study in Literary Psychology,* Psychological Monographs, XXXVII (1927), No. 1.

L'Esprit créateur, III (1963), Fall number. Entire issue devoted to Gautier.

Faguet, Emile. *Etudes littéraires sur le dix-neuvième siècle.* Paris, 1887.

George, Albert J. *Short Fiction in France, 1800–1850.* Syracuse, 1964.

Guischard, John A. *Le Conte fantastique au XIXe siècle.* Montréal, 1947.

Henriot, Emile. "Théophile Gautier, poète," *Annales romantiques,* IX (1912), 161–87.

James, Henry. *French Poets and Novelists.* London, 1878.
Jasinski, René. *Les Années romantiques de Th. Gautier.* Paris, 1929.
Larguier, Léo. *Théophile Gautier.* Paris, 1948.
Lauret, René. "L'Ame romantique de Théophile Gautier," *MdF,* CXI (1911), 225–39.
Marcel, Henry. *Essai sur Théophile Gautier.* Paris, 1903.
Nerval, Gérard de. *Œuvres,* eds. Albert Béguin et Jean Richer. 2 vols. Paris, 1952–61.
Poulet, Georges. *Etudes sur le temps humain.* Paris. 1949.
———. "Théophile Gautier et le Second Faust," *RLC,* XXII (1948), 67–83.
———. *Trois essais de mythologie romantique.* Paris, 1966.
Richardson, Joanna. *Théophile Gautier: His Life and Times.* New York, 1959.
Robert, Paul. *Dictionnaire alphabétique et analogique de la langue française.* 6 vols. Paris, 1951–64.
Sainte-Beuve, Charles-Augustin. *Nouveaux lundis.* 13 vols. Paris, 1865–86.
Schneider, Marcel. *La Littérature fantastique en France.* Paris, 1964.
Spoelberch de Lovenjoul, Charles de. *Histoire des œuvres de Théophile Gautier.* 2 vols. Paris, 1887.
Tild, Jean, *Théophile Gautier et ses amis.* Paris, 1951.
van der Tuin, H. *L'Evolution psychologique, esthétique et littéraire de Théophile Gautier.* Paris, 1933.
Vax, Louis. *L'Art et la littérature fantastiques.* Paris, 1963.
Velthuis, Henriette E. A. *Théophile Gautier: l'homme, l'artiste.* Middleburg, 1924.

UNIVERSITY OF FLORIDA MONOGRAPHS

Humanities

No. 1: *Uncollected Letters of James Gates Percival,* edited by Harry R. Warfel

No. 2: *Leigh Hunt's Autobiography: The Earliest Sketches,* edited by Stephen F. Fogle

No. 3: *Pause Patterns in Elizabethan and Jacobean Drama,* by Ants Oras

No. 4: *Rhetoric and American Poetry of the Early National Period,* by Gordon E. Bigelow

No. 5: *The Background of The Princess Casamassima,* by W. H. Tilley

No. 6: *Indian Sculpture in the John and Mable Ringling Museum of Art,* by Roy C. Craven, Jr.

No. 7: *The Cestus. A Mask,* edited by Thomas B. Stroup

No. 8: *Tamburlaine, Part I, and Its Audience,* by Frank B. Fieler

No. 9: *The Case of John Darrell: Minister and Exorcist,* by Corinne Holt Rickert

No. 10: *Reflections of the Civil War in Southern Humor,* by Wade H. Hall

No. 11: *Charles Dodgson, Semeiotician,* by Daniel F. Kirk

No. 12: *Three Middle English Religious Poems,* edited by R. H. Bowers

No. 13: *The Existentialism of Miguel de Unamuno,* by José Huertas-Jourda

No. 14: *Four Spiritual Crises in Mid-Century American Fiction,* by Robert Detweiler

No. 15: *Style and Society in German Literary Expressionism,* by Egbert Krispyn

No. 16: *The Reach of Art: A Study in the Prosody of Pope,* by Jacob H. Adler

No. 17: *Malraux, Sartre, and Aragon as Political Novelists,* by Catharine Savage

No. 18: *Las Guerras Carlistas y el Reinado Isabelino en la Obra de Ramón del Valle-Inclán,* por María Dolores Lado

No. 19: *Diderot's Vie de Sénèque: A Swan Song Revised,* by Douglas A. Bonneville

No. 20: *Blank Verse and Chronology in Milton,* by Ants Oras

No. 21: *Milton's Elisions,* by Robert O. Evans

No. 22: *Prayer in Sixteenth-Century England,* by Faye L. Kelly

No. 23: *The Strangers: The Tragic World of Tristan L'Hermite,* by Claude K. Abraham

No. 24: *Dramatic Uses of Biblical Allusion in Marlowe and Shakespeare,* by James H. Sims

No. 25: *Doubt and Dogma in Maria Edgeworth,* by Mark D. Hawthorne

No. 26: *The Masses of Francesco Soriano,* by S. Philip Kniseley

No. 27: *Love as Death in The Iceman Cometh,* by Winifred Dusenbury Frazer

No. 28: *Melville and Authority,* by Nicholas Canaday, Jr.

No. 29: *Don Quixote: Hero or Fool? A Study in Narrative Technique,* by John J. Allen

No. 30: *Ideal and Reality in the Fictional Narratives of Théophile Gautier,* by Albert B. Smith